EXECUTIVE EDITORS
Sarah Galbraith, Alan Doan,
Jenny Doan, David Mifsud

MANAGING EDITOR
Natalie Earnheart

CREATIVE DIRECTOR
Christine Ricks

PHOTOGRAPHER
BPD Studios

CONTRIBUTING PHOTOGRAPHER
Katie Whitt

VIDEOGRAPHER
Jake Doan

DESIGNER & TECHNICAL WRITER
Linda Johnson

PROJECT DESIGN TEAM
Natalie Earnheart, Jenny Doan,
Sarah Galbraith

CONTRIBUTING COPY WRITERS
Katie Mifsud, Jenny Doan, Hillary
Sperry, Natalie Earnheart, Christine
Ricks, Alan Doan, Sarah Galbraith

COPY EDITOR
Geoff Openshaw

CONTRIBUTING PIECERS
Jenny Doan, Natalie Earnheart,
Stephen Nixdorf, Cassie Nixdorf,
Cindy Morris

CONTRIBUTING QUILTERS
Bernice Kelly, Deloris Burnett, Jamey
Stone, Kathleen Miller, Betty Bates,
Adrian Stacey, Emma Jensen, Sherry
Melton, Cassie Martin, Amber Weeks,
Sandy Gaunce, Daniela Kirk, Amy
Gertz, Patty St. John,

CONTACT US
Missouri Star Quilt Co
114 N Davis
Hamilton, Mo. 64644
888-571-1122
info@missouriquiltco.com

6 COLOR CO-OP

10 LOVE NOTES

32 LATTICE

16 MINI PERIWINKLE

24 WONKY STAR

40 FREESTYLE STAR

content

DISAPPEARING PINWHEEL 48

FALLING CHARM 58

80 JACOBS LADDER

JELLY ROLL RACE 2 66

JENNY'S CLASSROOM 88

GARDEN PARTY 72

HELLO
from MSQC

Introducing BLOCK by Missouri Star Quilt Company. This is our first issue of this magazine and we are so excited to give it to you! BLOCK is a magazine we designed, produced, and published all in-house here at MSQC! We've taken the tutorials that we have done on our YouTube channel and transformed them into a great, easy-to-use magazine full of photos, ideas, and patterns. We hope it's an inspiring and easy to use guide to help you with your quilting projects!

We love everything about this: the new fabric, the photos, the layout, even the shape of the magazine is unique—in the shape of a quilt block! It's something we don't see out there anywhere else. As usual, each pattern or idea in here has an accompanying tutorial online. You get the best of both worlds! Not to mention we cut the price of our magazine by 40% so you could enjoy its benefits without it hurting your wallet (we are really good at being scrappy!). We are really happy with it, and are sure you will be, too! We hope BLOCK will inspire you to create beautiful quilts. Thanks for being a part of this exciting new venture.

Jenny

JENNY DOAN
MISSOURI STAR QUILT CO

“ We hope our magazine— BLOCK will inspire you to create beautiful quilts. ”

5

warming up to
WINTER

When I think of winter, my mind goes directly to my favorite cozy spot in my house—the couch next to my fireplace. I'll wrap myself up in one of my quilts and start a blazing fire in the fireplace. Add a good book and have my favorite pup curled up at my feet and I'm not moving for days.

Some of my fondest memories are winter days snowshoeing in the woods with my family, watching my gingerbread-colored dog leaping in the deep drifts and coming up with a face covered in white, blue skies and the yellow sun warming my cold red cheeks, grey woolly mittens, hand-knit by a friend, and my favorite almond tea to warm me at the end of the day. Winter can be hard with the shorter days and cold, dark nights. But living in the mountains I've come to learn to embrace the cold and even have its colors inspire me when I'm in need of something new to make.

Introducing BLOCKs Color Co-op! In every issue, we'll be gathering new groupings from our favorite fabrics that reflect the colors of the season. Be inspired to think of color in a new way! We here at MSQC hope this will kindle the creativity inside each of you.

CHRISTINE RICKS
MSQC Creative Director, BLOCK MAGAZINE

SOLIDS

FBY1168 Bella Solids White
by Moda
SKU# 9900 98

FBY3687 Kona Cotton Cream
by Robert Kaufman
SKU# K001-1090

FBY1687 Bella Solids Green
by Moda
SKU #9900 65

FBY3206 Bella Solids Home Town Sky
by Moda Fabrics
SKU# 9900 177

FBY1772 Bella Solids Teal
by Moda
SKU#9900 87

FBY9391 Cotton Supreme Solids Grey
by RJR
SKU# 9617-125

FBY3253 Kona Cotton Espresso
by Robert Kaufman
SKU# K001-1136

PRINTS

FBY9634 Muslin Mates by Moda
SKU# 9970 11

FBY8951 Moda Essential Dots Rose
by Moda
SKU# 8654 14

FBY9741 Wrens & Friends
by Gina Martin for Moda
SKU# 10005 13

FBY9126 Sweet Serenade
by BasicGrey for Moda
SKU# 30342 13

FBY6306 In My Room
by Jenean Morrison for Free Spirit
SKU# PWJM073

FBY10236 True Colors
by Joel Dewberry for Free Spirit
SKU# PWTC008

FBY3746 Tavern Blues
by Paula Barnes for Marcus
SKU# R22 4053 0113

LOVE notes

quilt designed by NATALIE EARNHEART

"Kindness" has many synonyms: words like love, service, or charity.

But I like the word "kindness" because it implies action. It

seems like something you and I can do. Acts of kindness reach

both the giver and the receiver, enlarging the souls of both.

I remember the days when we used to send love letters through the regular mail, how we would draw pictures or make our own cards. The written word is something we are in danger of losing. I wrote "XOXO" on a card and had to explain to one of my grandchildren what that meant. For those of you who don't know, it means a hug and a kiss.

When I was a young girl, we loved the mailman! We would wait not-so-patiently for the mail to arrive. It seemed all good things would arrive in the mailbox.

My mother and grandmother were wonderful examples to me. They both had friends and loved ones they would write letters to on a weekly basis. When my mother was about eight years old, she began writing a girl her age who lived in Hawaii through a pen pal program at school. They developed a wonderful friendship, and continued this correspondence throughout their adult years. They finally met face to face when they were in their seventies. It was a lovely culmination of a lasting relationship that was forged through the power of the written word.

When my mother would receive one of her special letters she would place this cherished piece of paper into a basket that she called "the basket of love." Every note she received, every child-scrawled drawing, or hand-written card, every love letter from my dad and all things in between went into the basket of love. Then if she ever had a sad day or just needed some cheering up, she would go to her basket of love and find the comforting sweet messages that would keep her spirits up. The words "I love you," and "Thank you," are like a balm for the soul. They transform tears into happiness. They provide comfort to the weary, and they confirm the tender feelings of our heart.

SEE THIS QUILT CREATED
in an alternate size using layer cakes.
You can find a link to Jenny's tutorial
in the resource section pg. 99

" When I read those emails or get a card it just makes my day. "

Now as an adult myself, I have also saved the cards and sweet messages I have received over the years. I have my own basket of love that I go to when I am having a sad day or need some words of encouragement or uplift. From the first days of starting our business I began to receive letters from all over the world and that love is such an amazing blessing for me. I just can't explain the way the written word can carry those sweet emotions. They lift, encourage, and inspire. When I read those emails or get a card, it just makes my day.

We all need to share the love and gratitude we feel with those around us. This quilt is a great combination of the written words of love combined with the comfort of a handmade quilt. The gift of a quilt is one of service, joy and love - a lasting gift that can be among the most memorable and appreciated of all gifts.

11

materials

makes a 39" x 50" charm pack quilt

QUILT TOP

- 1 printed charm pack
- 1 background solid charm pack
- ⅜ yd inner border
- ¾ yd outer border

BINDING

- ½ yd coordinating fabric

BACKING

- 1⅝ yds coordinating fabric

SAMPLE QUILT

- **Surrounded By Love** by Deb Strain for Moda Fabrics
- **Bella Solids Bleached White** by Moda Fabrics

1 sew

Pair two charm squares RST (right sides together)—one background solid, one print. Sew a ¼" seam around the edge.

You can stop and turn a quarter inch before the end or simply sew off the end—your choice.

2 cut

Cut across the charm squares diagonally twice. Sometimes this step goes faster with a rotating cutting mat.
YIELD: 4 HSTs (half square triangles)

Press seams to the darker side. Repeat 36 times.

3 construct

Arrange 3 HSTs of the same print and 1 of another print to create an envelope. Follow the diagram.

1 pair up RST

2 sew ¼" around the outside.
cut diagonally twice.

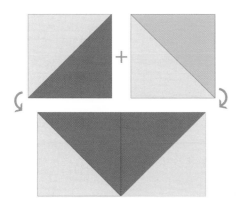

3 construct envelope

Join the top 2 HSTs together; then the bottom 2 HSTs. Press seams in opposite directions. Join top and bottom rows nesting seams to make one block. Repeat.

BLOCK SIZE: 5¾" square
YIELD: 36 blocks (use only 35)

4 arrange & sew

Lay out blocks in an eye-pleasing fashion using a 5 x 7 format. All the envelopes must face the same direction.

Sew blocks into rows. Press all seams in a row to the same side; all seams in the next row to the opposite side. This practice will help in nesting seam allowances. Follow arrows. Join rows to complete quilt center. Quilt center size: approx. 26¾" x 37¼"

TIP: *make sure envelopes face the same direction.*

5 inner border

Cut (4) 2½" strips of background fabric for the inner border. The following steps will help keep your quilt square and flat. Start with the top and bottom edges.

Measure the width of the quilt in three places: top edge, bottom edge and through the middle, folding the quilt in half widthwise to find the center.

Take the average of those 3 measurements. Piece strips together if needed. Cut 2 strips to the average measurement.

Stitch one of these measured strips to the top edge RST.**A** The border fabric should be on top as you sew. This method reduces wavy borders.

Always press to the borders. Repeat for the bottom edge.**B**

Follow the same procedure for both sides. Include the newly attached top & bottom borders in your measurements and this time fold in half lengthwise. **C & D**

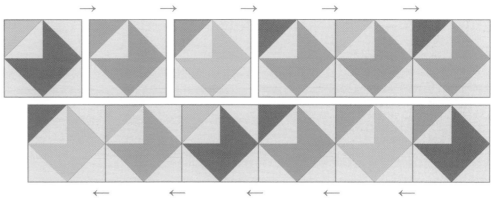

4 arrange envelopes. press seams to one side, and opposite side for next row.

13

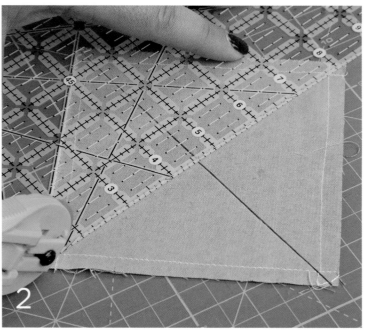

1   You will want to cut diagonally across your sewn together charm squares.

2   It's best not to move the block once you've started cutting. If you don't have a rotating cutting mat, use a smaller mat that you can pick up and turn for your second cut.

3   The envelope uses 3 half square triangles that are the same and one that is different. The illusion of an opened envelope is created. You are now ready to sew your block together.

> " I have my own basket of love that I go to when I am having a sad day or need some words of encouragement. "

6 outer border

Cut (4) 4½" strips of fabric for the outer border. Add to the quilt in the same manner the inner border was attached.

7 quilt & bind

Layer quilt top on batting and backing and quilt the way you like. Square up all raw edges.

Cut (5) 2½" strips of binding and piece together end-to-end with diagonal seams.

Fold in half lengthwise, press. Attach to your quilt raw edges together with a quarter inch seam allowance.

Turn the folded binding edge to the back and tack in place with an invisible stitch or machine stitch if you like.

FINISHED SIZE: approx. 39" x 50"

5 inner border
6 outer border

mini
Periwinkle
my antique inspiration

quilt designed by NATALIE EARNHEART

Collecting lost antiques has become a passion of mine. Being the first in two generations to quilt, I don't have any special family heirlooms and I love, LOVE old quilts. Gathering them has become a passion of mine. So when a couple of elderly women came into my shop and asked me if I would be interested in buying some quilts, of course I said YES! I was anxious to see what they had. We went out to their car and there in the back seat was a treasure trove of amazing quilts.

As for the two elderly women bearing quilting gifts, I learned they were sisters. Maxine and Ernestine grew up with their parents on a

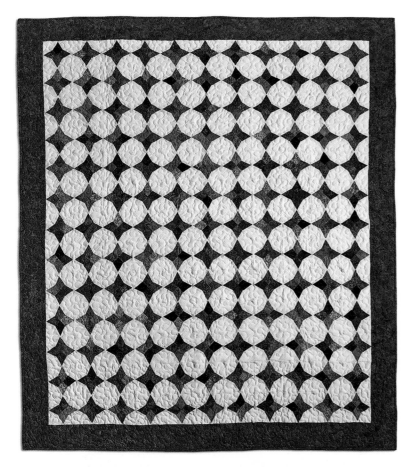

farm. Neither one ever married and they knew they wouldn't live forever. So they decided to find a home for these quilts that their mother had made for them. Her name was Lottie and that woman was a wonderful quilter! The piecing and stitching were perfect. You could see the quality, beauty and care that went into every stitch.

But even more amazing because these women were sisters, their mother made a quilt for each of them. They had two of everything! Talk about dedication. Right away I fell in love with the quilts and these ladies. I gladly purchased what they brought to sell. Now these quilts hang in my studio and remind me every day what a precious gift life is and what a wonderful life I lead.

One of those quilts was made in a beautiful star pattern that the ladies called "Periwinkle." When we asked our local expert if she knew anything about this quilt, she said she had seen the quilt before but never heard it called by that name. After a bit of research she came in and said she had found it in a 1929 Wallace Farmers Almanac with the name "Periwinkle." A short time later, while working in the studio, Natalie was looking at the periwinkle quilt and said, "I know how to make this without Y seams. It will be so much easier." That is how the Periwinkle quilt idea began. We have it in large and small templates and the quilts work up easily. All of this thanks to those two sweet sisters who shared their wonderful heirlooms with me!

LOTTIE KORDIS— she was a wonderful quilter and mother to Maxine and Ernestine.

19

materials

makes a 67" x 77" jelly roll quilt

QUILT TOP
- 1 jelly roll for periwinkles OR 4 charm packs
- 7½ yds background fabric
- 1 yd outer border

BINDING
- ⅝ yd coordinating fabric

BACKING
- 4¼ yds coordinating fabric

TOOLS
- MSQC mini wacky web template tool
- 3 packets small triangle papers
- glue stick

SAMPLE QUILT
- **Lagoon Batiks** by Jinny Beyer for RJR
- **Bella Solids White** by Moda Fabrics (9900 98)

1 CUT

Use the Mini Wacky Web Tool from MSQC (Missouri Star Quilt Company) to cut (572) "kites" from the charm squares, scraps or jelly roll—whichever you decide to use. 2½" square shown.

2 CONSTRUCT

Glue one kite right side up to a piece of triangle paper. The top of the kite should fit into the 90° corner of the paper triangle.

3 cut

Cut (104) 2½" background jelly roll strips; subcut into 3½" rectangles.

TOTAL 1144

1   Line up at least one side of the tool to a straight edge of fabric. Cut around the template to make a "kite."

2   Glue the kite onto the triangle paper matching the 90 degree angles to each other.

3   RST, line up to a side of the kite. The short side of a background rectangle to the side of the kite. Sew a ¼″ seam along this edge.

4   After pressing the first rectangle into place, proceed with the second leg of the kite.

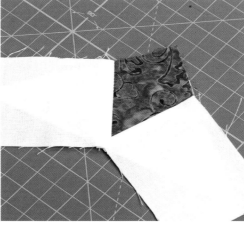

5   Your block should look like this once you've pressed the second leg into place.

6   Turn the entire unit upside down. Use the triangle paper as a pattern and trim off the excess fabric on 3 sides.

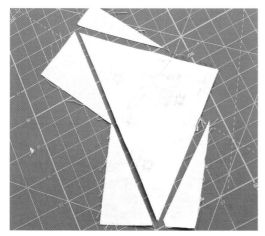

7   The unit is still upside down. These are the pieces you've trimmed away and you've gotten back to the original triangle shape.

8   Tear away the triangle paper. It will tear easily at the stitching line.

9   Each periwinkle is made up of 4 triangle units. Sew 2 adjacent sides together first; Press the seams in opposite directions; then sew those 2 larger units to each other. Nest the middle seam.

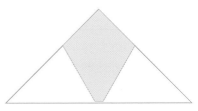

2 glue kite to triangle paper

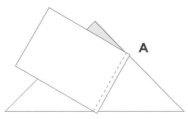

A

4 add sides

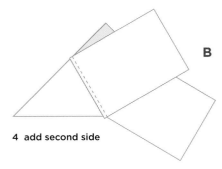

B

4 add second side

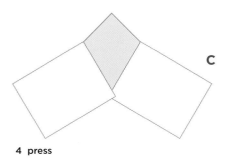

C

4 press

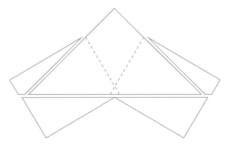

5 flip & trim

4 sew

RST (right sides together) sew a rectangle to one side of the kite with a ¼″ seam allowance. Press open. Repeat for the other leg of the kite. **A** & **B** Press open. **C**

Make 572

5 trim

Flip the kite unit over and trim excess background fabric using the triangle paper as a pattern. Remove the paper backing.

6 block

Piece 4 kite units together to make a periwinkle block. Match seams as you go. Nest the middle seams to complete the block.

Make 143

7 layout & sew

Lay the blocks into a 11 x 13 grid mixing colors in an eye-pleasing fashion. Sew blocks together across to build rows; then rows together to complete quilt center. Quilt Center: approx. 57½″ x 67½″

 TIP: *Position lights and darks next to each other in each block. It will be easier to balance color value over the entire quilt when laying it out.*

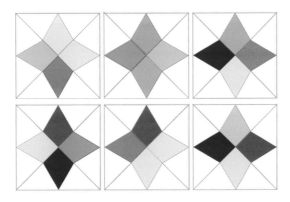

8 outer border

Cut (6) 5″ strips of border fabric. Piece together end-to-end as necessary. Measure and attach to top and bottom; then both sides. A-D Press to borders.

9 quilt & bind

Layer quilt top on batting and backing and quilt the way you like. Square up all raw edges.

Cut (8) 2½″ strips from binding fabric and piece together end-to-end with diagonal seams, aka plus sign method.

Fold in half lengthwise, press. Attach to your quilt raw edges together with a ¼″ seam.

Turn the folded binding edge to the back and tack in place with an invisible stitch— or machine stitch if you like.

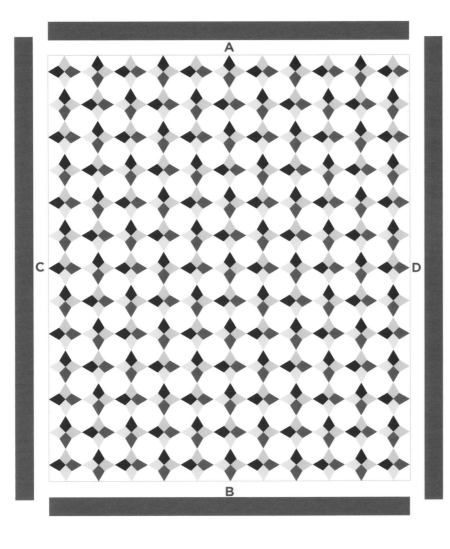

"...I fell in love with the quilts and these ladies."

speaking
WONKY
{stars that is}

quilt designed by NATALIE EARNHEART

Have you ever heard of a dead language? Latin, for example, is dead. Long gone. Extinct. Sure, there is the occasional scholar who is capable of carrying on a (probably one-sided) conversation in Latin, but you are about as likely to find a native Latin speaker as you are to come across a Tyrannosaurus Rex stomping around in your backyard.

English, on the other hand, is alive and well. And like pretty much all other living things, the English language is always growing and changing. Old words go out of style and are replaced with new words. What was once to referred to as "the bee's knees" later became "groovy," "cool," "gnarly" and, now, "epic."

New words are popping up all the time. Over the past few years Merriam-Webster has actually added several fun new words to the dictionary such as "unibrow," "drama queen,"

> " In my opinion, "Wonky Stars" is a much better quilt name than "Not in Correct Alignment Stars!" "

and "woot." Our language evolves and changes with each new generation. I have a cute four year old friend who has invented the term "yesternight." He'll often say something like, "Do you know what we had for dinner yesternight?" What a great new word! Who knows, maybe "yesternight" will find its way into the dictionary in the coming years.

The word "wonky" showed up sometime around the year 1920. It is defined as "not in correct alignment." In my opinion, "Wonky Stars" is a much better quilt name than "Not in Correct Alignment Stars!" It creates the image of whimsical asymmetry, imperfect and unpredictable- a spot-on description of this unexpected and unique pattern. "Wonky Stars" is a quilt that truly looks as fun as it sounds.

Variety is the spice of life, and a wide array of words certainly adds to the richness and flavor of our speech. When you add the word "wonky" to wonderful things like a quilt pattern it makes them even better.

OUR WONKY STARS PATTERN is so versatile that it transitions easily into all different types of fabrics. From patriotic to every-day it will always look great!

materials

makes a 66" X 77" layer cake quilt

QUILT TOP
- 1 layer cake collection with duplicates of each fabric* OR 1 layer cake and 1 charm pack of the same collection (if the layer cake does not have duplicates)
- 1 layer cake solid
- ¾ yd inner border
- 1½ yd outer border

BINDING
- ¾ yd coordinating fabric

BACKING
- 4 yds 45" wide coordinating fabric OR 2 yds 90" wide coordinating fabric

SAMPLE QUILT
- **Belle** by Amy Butler for Rowan Fabrics (only 1 layer cake needed)

1 the block

Each star uses (13) 5" squares:
- 10 blocks of 5 print & 8 solid squares for print star
- 10 blocks of 8 print & 5 solid squares for solid star

4 layer cake squares required for each block: 2 solid, 2 print. Cut all layer cakes into 5" squares. 2 layer cake squares required of each print. Group 13 squares together in stacks for each type of star.

2 star leg

To make a star point for a block with a printed star, select 2 squares—1 print and 1 solid. Fingerpress a small fold at the bottom of the solid square marking the halfway point. Press. All seams are ¼".

Lay the squares RST (right sides together), positioning the print square to make the first leg of the star. Overlap the halfway point fold. Sew, flip and press.

1 The tan fabric shown will become the star leg. Make sure your seam allowance crosses the middle of the printed square's edge. Sew and press so the tan fabric covers the corner of the print square.

2 Work on the wrong side. Line up the corner of your ruler to the corner of the printed square that was covered by the tan fabric. Cut off the excess tan fabric being careful to preserve as much as possible for the next star leg.

3 Use what's left from the first cut to sew this piece for the second leg of the star.

4 Flip the unit over to the right side. Open the tan fabric to reveal the original sewing line. Trim off excess print fabric using the tan fabric as a guide.

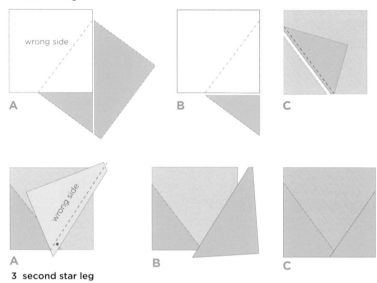

2 trim star leg

A

B

C

A

B

C

3 second star leg

Turn the unit upside down. Trim off excess star fabric. Make 2 cuts **A** & **B** using the background square as the cutting guide. Flip the unit to the right side, open star fabric and trim excess ¼" from sewing line. **C**

3 second star leg

Use the larger scrap piece from 2**A** to create the second star point. Place RST and cross over the star fabric at or above ¼" seam allowance. The red dot indicates ¼."**A** Sew. Press open. Flip and trim to the background square as in 2**A** & **B**. Flip to the front, trim excess fabric as in 2**C**. Make 4.

BLOCK SIZE: 5" x 5"

4 make star block

With the 4 star point blocks and the remaining 5 squares, arrange the star. Sew blocks across in rows, then rows down to create the block. Nest the seams as you go. Note the pressing arrows.

BLOCK SIZE: 14" x 14"
Make 20

5 layout & sew

Arrange the blocks in a 4 x 5 grid. Sew blocks together into rows first. Press all seams to one side on even rows; to the opposite side on odd rows. This will help with nesting. Sew rows together to create the quilt center.

6 borders

Cut (8) 2½" strips for the inner border. Measure quilt center width and cut 2 strips to that length. Attach to top and bottom. **A** & **B** Repeat for quilt sides. **C** & **D** Cut (8) 6" strips for the outer border. Attach in the same fashion.

7 quilt & bind

Layer quilt top on batting and backing and quilt the way you like. Square up all raw edges.

Cut (8) 2½" strips. Piece together end-to-end with diagonal seams - aka plus sign method.

Fold in half lengthwise, press.

Attach to your quilt raw edges together with a ¼" seam allowance. Turn the folded binding edge to the back and tack in place with an invisible stitch—or machine stitch if you like.

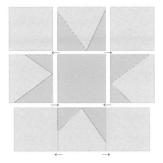

4 make star block

5 sew quilt center

6 add borders

Lattice Quilt

by way of the front porch

quilt designed by JENNY DOAN

Some quilts are born from an idea for a pattern; others are inspired by the fabrics. Some require a bit of both, and that is part of the story of this quilt! I have been wanting to make a lattice quilt for a few years and I just haven't had the fabric that made that quilt want to fly out of my fingers. This year I got some fabric from Moda. I love Jan Patek's line of fabrics, but this one was named FRONT PORCH. It was the name that really got me. I thought about front porches that have lattice fencing with flowers weaving through it and before I knew it, this quilt was born!

> "Porches come in all shapes and sizes, but what really matters are the memories that are made on that porch."

I have always had a house with a porch. That has been an important consideration for me in choosing a place to live. The house I live in now won my heart with its big wrap-around porch.

So many wonderful things have taken place on this front porch. We have conversations, family photos, haircuts, talent shows, and everything in-between.

When we moved to this Victorian house, we set about fixing it up and the porch was the first thing. After repairing the porch, the whole house just straightened up!

After the house was finished, my boys put a skateboard ramp on the side of the porch, and they skated around the front to the side of the porch and up the ramp.

One day the town doctor came by to compliment us on how good the house looked and

*WE LOVE USING OUR QUILTS,
whether we are eating donuts,
making forts or just bundling up
on the front porch with them.*

asked, "Why would you allow those kids to skateboard on that beautiful porch?" I told him that my husband and I would probably sit alone on that porch for more than 40 years, so if they wanted to skate on it for the next 2 years it was ok with me. He looked a bit chagrined, smiled and said, "You are absolutely right."

Now the children are grown and have their own porches. Ron and I sit on our porch, cherishing the memories and looking forward to visits from grandkids who will undoubtedly make new memories on this very porch.

materials

makes a 71" x 67" lap quilt

QUILT TOP
• 4 charm packs OR 1 layer cake
• 1 honey bun solid OR 1 ¾ yd solid for lattice
• 1 yd outer border

BINDING
• ⅝ yd coordinating fabric

BACKING
• 4 yds coordinating fabric

SAMPLE QUILT
• **Front Porch** by Jan Patek for Moda Fabrics

1 cut

The quilt is made with 5" squares. If you are using a layer cake, cut all the squares in half twice. Cut (156) twice (4) 5" squares per layer cake in half diagonally.

FOR LATTICE:

If you are using fabric off the bolt, cut (32) 1½" strips. Subcut 1½" strips into (156) 8" rectangles.

2 iron

Fold the 2 triangles RST (right sides together) in half and iron or fingerpress a crease into the fabric. Fold a 1½" strip in half and press in a crease.

3 sew

Lay a triangle and strip RST. The peaks of the creases should nestle together; this keeps triangle and strip centered—which

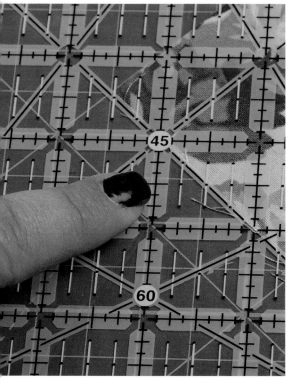

1 Cut through the square diagonally from corner to corner. Use the 45° angle marking on the ruler for a guide to a perfect cut.

2 Finger pressing a seam is an easy way to line center folds up without the hassle of an iron.

3 Fold your block in half through the middle of the lattice strip and trim both ends.

1 cut diagonally once

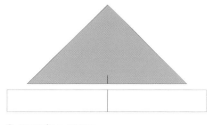

2 press in a crease

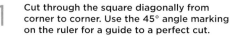

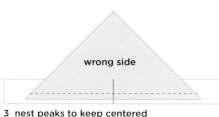

3 nest peaks to keep centered

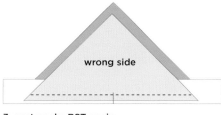

3 nest peaks RST again

is very important for this block. Pin in place. Sew a ¼" seam. Lay the next triangle of a different color on the opposite edge of the strip RST. Try to pair darks and lights. Allow the peaks to nestle; sew. Press seams toward the strip.

Make 156

4 trim

Fold the block diagonally in half down the center of the lattice strip. Iron. With a ruler trim the lattice strip on both ends using the edge of the triangles as a cutting guide.

5 layout

Lay out all the blocks in a 12 x 13 block grid. The lattice strips will follow a zig-zag pattern across the row. All even rows will begin the zig-zag in the opposite direction. Follow the diagram.

6 sew

Sew blocks together in rows first; then rows together to complete the quilt center. Nesting seams is possible at block intersections where no lattice strips connect.

7 borders

Cut (6) 1½″ strips of lattice fabric for the inner border. Measure and cut two lengths for the top & bottom quilt edges. Piece end-to-end as needed. Attach and press to border; repeat for both sides. **A-D**

Cut (7) 5″ strips of outer border fabric. Attach to quilt top in the same order the inner borders were attached.

8 quilt & bind

Layer quilt top on batting and backing and quilt the way you like. Square up all raw edges.

Cut (8) 2½″ strips from binding fabric and piece together end-to-end with diagonal seams, aka plus sign method.

Fold in half lengthwise, press. Attach to your quilt raw edges together with a ¼″ seam.

Turn the folded binding edge to the back and tack in place with an invisible stitch— or machine stitch if you like.

 TIP: *Here are two ways to achieve an even balance between light and dark overall in your quilt top.* **1** *Stand above the layed out blocks and squint.* **2** *Use a camera to take a picture—then turn it black & white so you only see value. Either method will help you avoid clumping too many lights or darks together.*

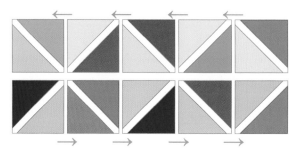

6 blocks into rows; sew rows together

7 attach borders

Freestyle Stars

quilt designed by NATALIE EARNHEART

I have an old quilt that I keep in the trunk of my car. It is tattered and stained here and there, but it is also worn to perfect softness and it smells like the sun of a hundred summer picnics. (Not to be overly dramatic, or anything...) I call it my adventure quilt. I made it as a gift for my husband on our first Christmas together along with an adorably mushy letter about all the wonderful places we would go and the things we would do together. Now, years later, we are also starting to look a little worn and tattered, but we've had many an adventure along the way, and more often than not, that quilt came right along with us.

There is something wonderful about a well-loved quilt. You're not afraid to really use it. You don't worry too much about rips or spills or grass stains. It becomes one of the most useful objects known to man. A worn out quilt is a tablecloth, a fort, and a comfy spot to lay and watch the stars. It's a towel at the beach, a superhero cape or a makeshift shelter in an unexpected rainstorm. Maybe most importantly, you never worry about kids on a well worn

quilt. I've pulled mine out of the trunk to cushion a little one getting an impromptu diaper change more than a few times!

When my kids were little, we loved to spread a quilt out on the front lawn in the late afternoon and wait for "Daddy" to come home. We brought along snacks of crackers, cheese and grapes. On library day we would read our newly borrowed books to pass the time. Each of the kids had a favorite square on the quilt and that was where they sat every time. My sweet girly-girl always claimed the bright pink square, my rough and tumble boy went for the navy blue. On chilly days we cuddled in the middle and pulled the edges up over our shoulders. On days that were downright cold or rainy, we stayed inside and created a fort with our blanket.

When I make a new quilt for a friend, I don't want it to be carefully tucked away like a delicate treasure. I want it to be used. I want it to see sun and rain and laughter. I want it to wrap them up in comfort and warmth. I want it to be as useful as it is beautiful. I will always love a pristine quilt carefully draped over my bed, or hung like a piece of art over the sofa. But as the years go by, I find that it's the quilts that were really used that I treasure most. That old quilt in my trunk may be threadbare and faded, but the memories it carries with it are more beautiful than any new quilt.

“ I want it to be used. I want it to see sun and rain and laughter. ”

 YOU CAN CHANGE THE ENTIRE LOOK OF A QUILT by adding sashing between the blocks. See Jenny's easy sashing tutorial in the reference section p.95!

materials

makes a 65" X 71" layer cake quilt

QUILT TOP
- 1 layer cake white
- 1 layer cake print
- 1¼ yd outer border

BINDING
- ⅝ yd coordinating fabric

BACKING
- 4 yds coordinating fabric

TOOLS
- MSQC large wedge ruler

SAMPLE QUILT
- **True Colors** by Joel Dewberry for Free Spirit Fabrics
- **Bella Solid White** by Moda Fabrics

1 create half square triangle

Pair two layer cakes RST (right sides together) for a total of 20 pairs. Sew a ¼" seam all around.

You can stop and turn a quarter inch before the end or simply sew off the end—your choice.

2 cut

Sometimes this step goes faster with a rotating cutting mat. Cut across the layer cake diagonally twice.

YIELD: 4 half square triangles (HSTs). Press seams to the darker side. Set the 4 HSTs aside in a stack together all facing the same direction. Repeat 20 times.

1 pair up RST & sew

2 cut diagonally twice

3 cut

From the solid white layer cakes cut 2 triangles from each using the Large Wedge Tool from Missouri Star Quilt Company. Remember to "put your wedge on the edge." Stack up to 4 at a time if you wish. Repeat for a total of 40 layer cake squares.

YIELD: 80 triangles.

4 add wedge

Fold a wedge in half down the center and iron. This gives you a sewing guide. Open wedge. Choose which color right triangle to align to. The top of the wedge aligns to the 90° corner of that colored triangle. Place onto the HST right sides together (RST). **A**

TIP: The wedge's fold must cross over the HST's seam.

Sew on the folded line. Repeat the exact positioning with the other 3 matching HSTs. Be consistent!

Keep the sewn wedge folded in half before the next step. Trim off the excess solid white wedge using the square HST as a guide. **B**

Open the wedge up. Trim ¼" from the sew line removing the excess fabric behind the wedge. **C** Press open.

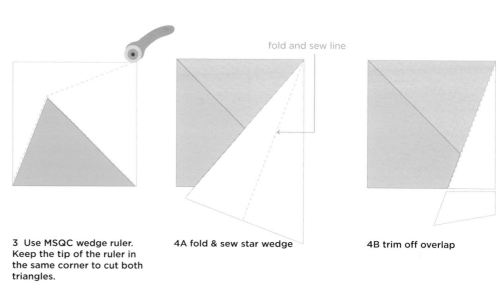

fold and sew line

3 Use MSQC wedge ruler. Keep the tip of the ruler in the same corner to cut both triangles.

4A fold & sew star wedge

4B trim off overlap

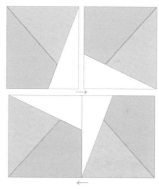

4C trim off excess white

5 build block

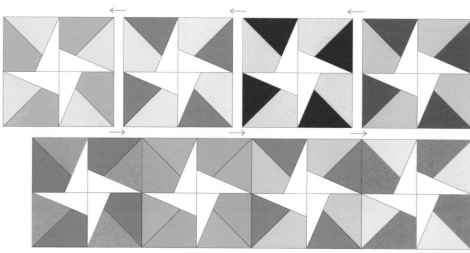

6 sew & nest seams

1 Make your first star triangle. Using the MSQC triangle ruler, cut from the bottom of the ruler edge (middle of square) to the top of the layer cake square. Notice the top tip of the triangle stays in the same corner for each triangle you cut.

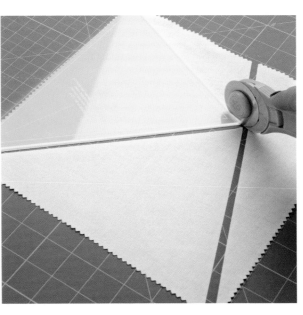

2 Lay the triangle ruler onto the other side of the half square cut you just made and cut the other side of the triangle.

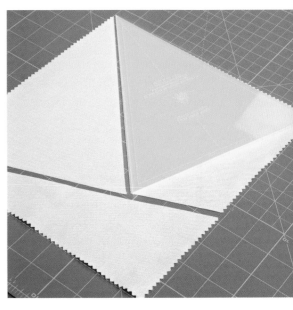

3 You should be able to get two triangles from the layer cake.

4 Press a fold down the center of the triangle. Position it on the HST making sure the fold crosses over both colors. Sew on the triangle fold line.

5 Fold the white triangle closed - away from the center. Align the ruler with the bottom edge of the HST and cut off the excess white triangle.

6 Open the triangle flat. Trim ¼" from the stitching line removing excess fabric from underneath the star leg.

A

C

D

B

7 add borders

5 build block

Build the wedge star block with 4 modified HSTs. All right-angled corners of the wedges will meet in the center.

Sew blocks together first side to side and then top to bottom. Press. Follow pressing arrows to aid in nesting seams. Repeat for all the modified HSTs.

YIELD: 20 wedge star blocks.

6 arrange & sew

Lay out blocks in an eye-pleasing fashion using a 4 x 5 format. Nest the center seams and sew the blocks together side by side to build a row. Follow the pressing arrows to aid in nesting seams. Sew rows together to complete quilt center. Nest seams.

7 outer border

Cut (7) 5″ strips of border fabric. Piece together end-to-end as necessary. Measure and attach to top and bottom; then both sides. **A-D** Press to borders.

8 quilt & bind

Layer quilt top on batting and backing and quilt the way you like. Square up all raw edges.

Cut (8) 2½″ strips from binding fabric and piece together end-to-end with diagonal seams, aka plus sign method.

Fold in half lengthwise, press. Attach to your quilt raw edges together with a ¼″ seam.

Turn the folded binding edge to the back and tack in place with an invisible stitch—or machine stitch if you like.

Disappearing Pinwheel

and getting inspired

quilt designed by JENNY DOAN

I'm always looking for fresh ideas for my quilting, and

director Alfred Hitchcock said that ideas come from

everything. But I don't know about everything. I mean,

I've never been inspired by, say, leftover tuna casserole.

But maybe I'm just not looking closely enough. It is

pretty amazing how simple things can spark big ideas.

Stuff falling over has inspired a surprising number of creative achievements. Composer William Gilbert (of Gilbert & Sullivan) got the idea for his wildly successful opera *The Mikado* when a Japanese sword fell off the wall where it was displayed in his study. I would probably be more terrified than inspired if that happened to me. But hey, maybe terror and inspiration can be one and the same. The screenwriter and director of horror film *Paranormal Activity* says he got the haunting idea for the movie when a box of detergent fell off a shelf for no apparent reason. Although *Paranormal Activity* isn't my cup of tea, I say good for him. That's one way to create something instead of just hiding under the covers!

So what does this mean for my quilting? Looking at these great achievers, I realize I'm not inspired by fear or by frustration. How can I find a way to get my creative juices flowing?

Maybe I'll take a page out of Jenny Doan's book. As she relaxed at the lakeside and considered other ways she had used a disappearing nine patch or a disappearing four patch, Jenny

came up with the adorable Disappearing Pinwheel pattern. If the serenity of an afternoon at the lake can result in a quilt like this, I'm booking myself a trip to Tahoe!

Whatever it is that gets your juices flowing, enjoy it! Who knows, maybe it will inspire you to try something different.

THE THING WE LOVE ABOUT the easy Disappearing Pinwheel is the one method makes two great quilts: the Shoofly and the Churn Dash. Just turn the block components one way or the other and get completely different quilts.

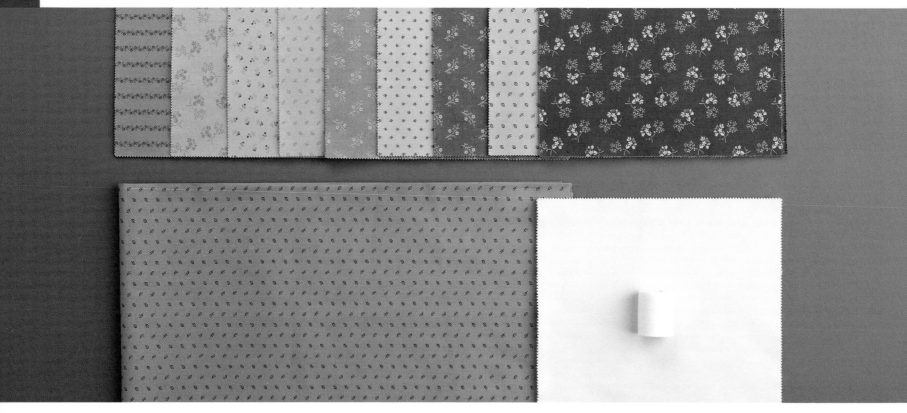

Our Disappearing Pinwheel pattern is a fun way to create two totally different quilts with just one technique! By rearranging the squares into different configurations you can make a quilt with two completely different looks. Try Shoofly for one look and Churn Dash for another.

shoofly materials

makes a 75 ¾" x 87" layer cake quilt

QUILT TOP
- 1 layer cake print
- 1 layer cake background solid
- 1 ¼ yd borders background solid

BINDING
- ⅝ yd coordinating fabric

BACKING
- 5 yds coordinating fabric

SAMPLE QUILT
- **Floral Gatherings** by Primitive Gatherings for Moda Fabrics
- **Bella Solids Natural** by Moda Fabrics

shoofly pattern

1 sew

Set aside 10 of the lightest colored print layer cakes for later use.

Pair two layer cakes RST (right sides together)—one light, one dark. Sew a ¼" seam all around. You can stop and turn a quarter inch before the end or simply sew off the end—your choice.

2 cut

Sometimes this step goes faster with a rotating cutting mat. With your rotary cutter cut across the layer cake diagonally twice.

YIELD: 4 half square triangles (HST). Press seams to the darker side. Repeat 30 times.

3 pinwheels

Arrange the 4 HSTs to create a pinwheel. Follow the diagram.

Sew HSTs in rows first RST. Press to the dark side. Sew the two rows together nesting seams as you go. **Make 30**

4 cut

Cut the pinwheel into 9 squares. Square up the pinwheel to 12¾." This will make cutting in thirds much easier. Each of the 9 squares will measure 4¼." Divided by 2 (=2⅛") this measurement will allow you to use the center seams to help with the cutting. Line up the ruler with a center seam. Cut 2⅛" from the center seam on all four sides. A rotating cutting mat comes in handy for this step.

1 pair up RST

2 cut diagonally twice

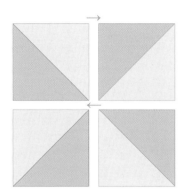

3 construct pinwheel

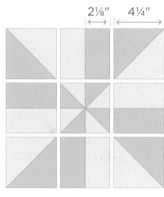

4 cut pinwheel

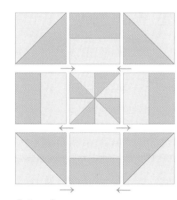

5 turn & sew

5 turn & sew

Turn each of the 8 outside squares to match the diagram. Sew the 3 blocks of each row together first. Press according to the arrows. Sew rows together nesting seams.

BLOCK SIZE: 11¾" x 11¾"
YIELD: 30 blocks

6 layout & sew

Layout the blocks in a 5 x 6 grid in an eye-pleasing fashion. Sew blocks together in rows; then rows together to form the quilt center. Follow pressing arrows for help in nesting seams.

7 inner border

Cut (7) 2½" strips of background fabric. Measure and attach 2 strips to top and bottom of quilt center. Piece strips together end-to-end when needed. Repeat for the quilt sides.

6 construct quilt center

7 add inner border

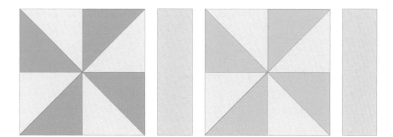

8 pieced border

 TIP: *Be aware of the differences in pieced border construction. Top & bottom borders begin & end with rectangles; side borders begin & end with pinwheels.*

1 Once you've squared up your pinwheel block to 12¾", cutting it into thirds is a cinch. Cut 2⅛" away from the center seam on both sides. Repeat for the other center seam. Do not move the fabric while cutting.

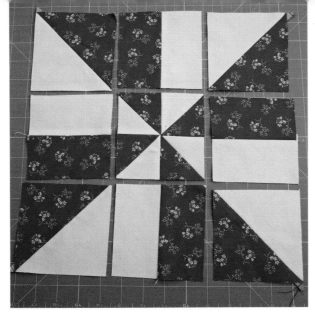

2 Pinwheel block cut into 9 equal segments.

3 Turn each corner block so the print is angled toward the center.

8 pieced border

Use the 10 light colored print layer cakes that were set aside in this step.

Cut 10 print and 10 background layer cakes into 5" squares. Use one print and one background square to make (38) pinwheels following steps 1, 2 & 3.

YIELD: (80) 5" squares from each group of layer cakes.

BLOCK SIZE APPROX: 5¾" x 5¾"

Cut (7) 2½" strips of inner border fabric. Subcut into (38) 2½" x 5¾" rectangles.

FOR TOP AND BOTTOM: piece 8 pinwheels and 9 rectangle strips together. Start and end with a 2½" rectangle strip. Make 2. Attach to quilt top and bottom.

FOR BOTH SIDES: use 11 pinwheels with 10 strips between them. Start and end with a pinwheel. Make 2. Attach to either side. You may need to ease the borders to fit properly.

APPROX SIZE: 71¼" x 82½" Turn the folded binding edge to the back and tack in place with an invisible stitch—or machine stitch if you like.

❝ Whatever it is that gets your juices flowing, enjoy it! ❞

churn dash materials
makes a 57" X 68" layer cake quilt

QUILT TOP
- 1 layer cake
- 1 yd outer border

BINDING
- ⅝ yd coordinating fabric

BACKING
- 3½ yds coordinating fabric

SAMPLE QUILT
- **Muslin Mates** by Moda Fabrics

churn dash pattern

1 sew
Pair two layer cakes RST (right sides together)—one background, one print. Sew a ¼" seam all around.

You can stop and turn a quarter inch before the end or simply sew off the end–your choice.

2 cut
Sometimes this step goes faster with a rotating cutting mat. With your rotary cutter cut across the layer cake diagonally twice.

YIELD: 4 half square triangles (HST). Press seams to the darker side. Repeat 10 times in high contrasting layer cake pairs; 10 times in low contrasting layer cake pairs.

3 pinwheels
Arrange the 4 HSTs to create a pinwheel. Follow the diagram.

Sew HSTs in rows first RST. Press to the dark side. Sew the two rows together nesting seams as you go.

Make 20

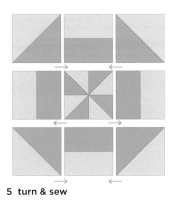

5 turn & sew

4 cut

Cut the pinwheel into 9 squares: Square up the pin-wheel to 12¾." This will make cutting in thirds much easier. Each of the 9 squares will measure 4¼." Divided by 2 (=2⅛") this measurement will allow you to use the center seams to help with the cutting. Line up the ruler with the center seam. Cut 2⅛" from the center seam on all four sides. A rotating cutting mat comes in handy for this step.

5 turn & sew

Turn each of the 8 outside squares to match the diagram. Sew 3 blocks of each row together first. Press according to the arrows. Sew rows together nesting seams.

BLOCK SIZE: 11¾" x 11¾"
YIELD: 10 blocks high contrast, 10 blocks low contrast

6 layout & sew

Layout the blocks in a 4 x 5 grid in an eye-pleasing fashion. Alternate dark and light blocks. Sew blocks together in rows; then rows together to form the quilt center. Follow pressing arrows to aid in nesting seams.

7 outer border

Cut (7) 6" strips of border fabric. Piece together end-to-end as necessary. Measure and attach to top and bottom; then both sides. **A-D**

8 quilt & bind

Layer quilt top on batting and backing and quilt the way you like. Square up all raw edges.

Cut (7) 2½" strips and piece together end-to-end with diagonal seams–plus sign method.

Fold in half lengthwise, press. Attach to your quilt raw edges together with a ¼" seam.

Turn the folded binding edge to the back and tack in place with an invisible stitch—or machine stitch if you like.

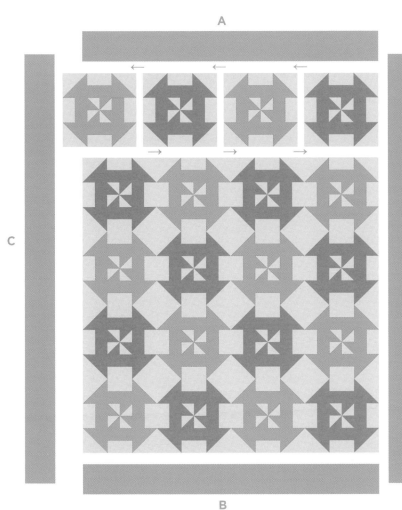

6 construct quilt center
7 add border

Falling for a charm quilt

quilt designed by JENNY DOAN

I have a quilt that my grandmother made as a present for my high school graduation. I love it. I love that I can imagine her small, capable hands skillfully sewing every stitch. I love that the quilt represents the love and warmth I always felt when I was with her. But if I'm being really honest, I don't actually love the look of the quilt. Dusty mauves and mature florals in a traditional flower basket pattern are a perfect match for my grandma's house, but they look absolutely out of place in my more contemporary home. That's why I was thrilled to learn about the modern movement in quilting. It blends the generations-old tradition of quilting with the style of today. I have been able to take the skills I learned from my grandma and combine them with my own sense of style to create quilts that really represent who I am.

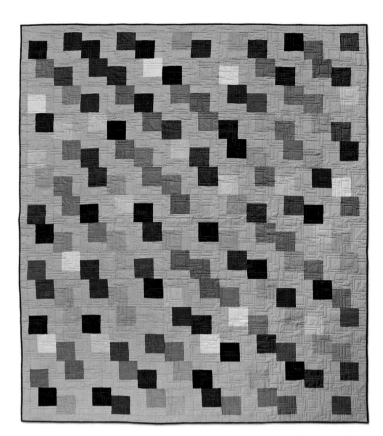

Of course quilting style is as individual and varied as taste in fashion, art, or food. Some like bold colors, some muted. Some prefer busy, patterned fabrics, others like to stick with solids or simple motifs. Some cling to the time-tested designs of traditional quilting, and some love the style innovations of modern quilting.

Modern quilting can really be anything that branches out from tradition. One of the hottest trends in modern quilting is the use of solid fabrics. Solid fabrics are fun because they really allow the piecing to shine. The focus is all on color and shape. Because of the simplicity of the fabric, the eye is drawn to details that might be missed with busier fabric.

Other common markers of modern quilting include: large amounts of negative space, unexpected scale, and bold prints. Of course, a modern quilter may use all or none of these elements. The important thing is that she feels free to break from tradition and create something unique and beautiful that is all her own. After all, a quilt truly is a piece of art that reflects the aesthetic and imagination of the artist.

Whether you are a quilter that loves to experiment with new styles and methods or you prefer to stick to tradition, one thing is sure: Modern quilting has caused the art to become attractive to a wider audience. Modern quilting allows tradition and innovation to be stitched together in new and wonderful ways.

materials

makes a 83" X 96" charm pack quilt

QUILT TOP
- 4 charm packs OR 1 layer cake
- 2 jelly rolls background solid

BINDING
- ¾ yd coordinating fabric

BACKING
- 7½ yds coordinating fabric

SAMPLE QUILT
- **Weave** by Moda Fabrics
- **Bella Solids Silver** by Moda Fabrics (9900 183)

If you purchased a layer cake, cut each 10" square into (4) 5" squares.

1 construct block

The block consists of (1) 5" charm square with (2) jelly roll strips bordering two adjacent sides. Add the first side to the charm square without cutting the jelly roll. Here's how:

At the sewing machine, lay the jelly roll strip face up ready to sew lengthwise. Place a 5" charm square face down on top, right sides together (RST). Sew a ¼" seam. When you come to the end of a charm square, place another on the strip leaving a bit of a gap; about 8 squares per strip.

Cut the strip sets apart, trimming any excess as you go. Press to the jelly roll. Use the same method for the adjacent side.

BLOCK: 7" x 7"
Make 168

1 Stitch 5" squares to 2½" strips.

2 Trim off excess fabric.

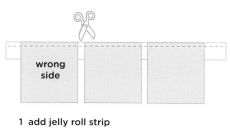

1 add jelly roll strip

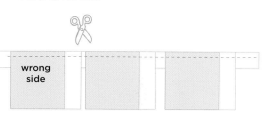

1 Cut apart and trim off excess.
Add another strip to the adjacent side.

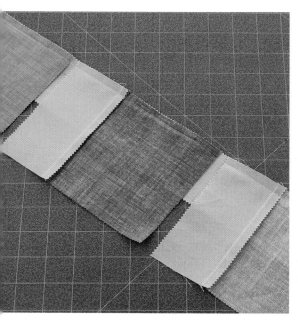

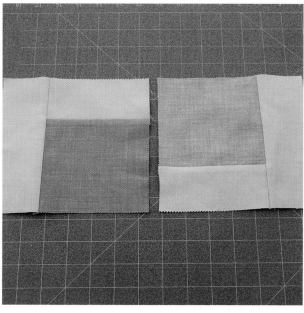

3 Sew a sashing strip between flower blocks.

4 The cornerstone in the sashing between rows will line up with the sashing that's between blocks.

2 layout

Blocks are arranged in a 12 x 14 grid in an eye-pleasing fashion, positioned in 2 orientations: corner upper right, and corner lower left. Alternate within the row and from row to row.

3 sew

Stitch blocks together to form rows. Follow pressing arrows. This makes nesting seams easier. Sew rows together nesting seams as you go. Press seams toward the bottom.

QUILT CENTER: approx. 78½" x 91½"

4 border

Cut (9) 2½" strips for the inner border. Measure top and bottom. Piece strips together end-to-end as necessary. Attach to top and bottom; repeat for both sides. **A—D** Press to borders.

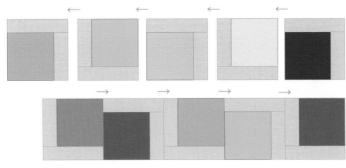

3 sew blocks into rows; press;
  sew rows together; press

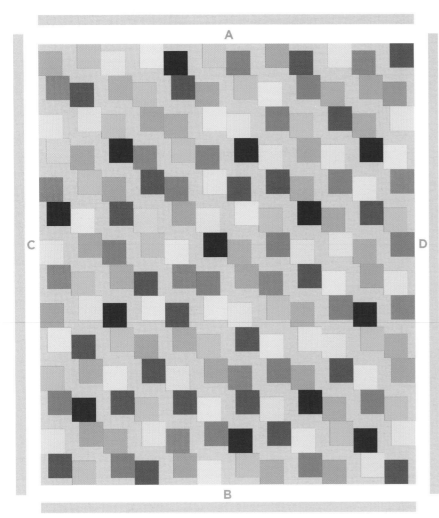

4 attach border

> " Modern quilting can really be anything that branches out from tradition. Solid fabrics are fun because they really allow the piecing to shine. "

5 quilt & bind

Layer quilt top on batting and backing and quilt the way you like. Square up all raw edges.

Cut (9) 2½" strips from binding fabric and piece together end-to-end with diagonal seams, aka plus sign method. Fold in half lengthwise, press. Attach to the quilt raw edges together with a ¼" seam.

Turn the folded binding edge to the back and tack in place with an invisible stitch or machine stitch if you like.

Jelly Roll Race 2

small changes = big results

quilt designed by SARAH GALBRAITH

My father was a big fan of New Year's resolutions. Every year on the first Monday in January he would gather us all into the living room. We took turns reading out loud our list of goals from the previous year. It was great fun booing and cheering each others' failures and successes. At the end of the night we would spend some time writing down goals for the new year.

Year after year we started with great excitement, but as the weeks went by, our determination faded until eventually our New Year's resolutions were pretty much forgotten.

I often think back to my first (failed) attempt at quilting. I was 15 years old and full of energy and creativity. I carefully selected a lovely assortment of starred, striped, and solid fabrics in a patriotic palette of red, white, and blue. The quilt pattern was one I had discovered in a quilting calendar at my grandmother's house. It was an intricate design of small triangles and teeny, tiny squares.

THE JELLY ROLL RACE IS A REALLY EASY QUILT, some gals can do this entire top in under an hour! Try doing a Jelly Roll Race at your next guild meeting!

I painstakingly cut out each square with my new rotary cutter, determined to obtain geometric perfection. Every seam was carefully pressed, every thread neatly clipped. My quilt was destined to be the very essence of flawless beauty. But then . . .I gave up.

Looking back, I'm sure it was the tiny squares that did me in. It seemed that no matter how many perfect little squares I pieced together, the quilt never got any larger. Hours upon hours of careful work had yielded nothing more than a few feet of finished quilt top. I was frustrated. I was bored. I packed it all up in a box, stuck it in the top of my closet, and quickly forgot about the failed project all together.

One decade later, I was a newly married young adult anxiously awaiting the arrival of my first child. At the

<blockquote>
" I've learned a thing or two about achieving my goals, and I think the key is: keep it simple. "
</blockquote>

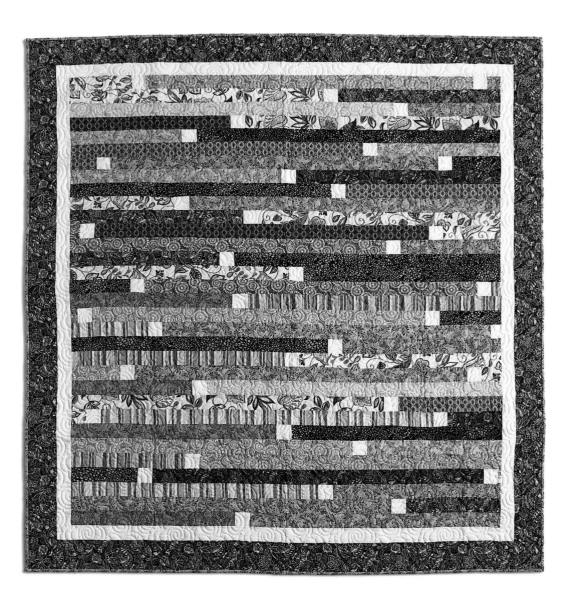

baby shower, my mother surprised me with a very unexpected gift: my long forgotten quilt. She had taken the portion I had completed, and cleverly added just enough to create the most beautiful little baby quilt I had ever seen.

Mom's creativity taught me a great lesson. My 15-year-old self would have been much more successful with my first-ever quilting project if I'd made just a small change or two. I could have chosen a simpler pattern or enlarged the scale of the pattern I loved. I could have done what my mother did and settled for a smaller—but completed—finished product.

Over the years I've learned a thing or two about achieving my goals, and I think the key is: keep it simple. Success is so much more obtainable when we resolve to make bite-sized adjustments to our everyday lives. Small changes can produce wonderful transformations.

materials

makes a 71" X 79" jelly roll quilt

QUILT TOP
- 1 jelly roll
- 1 yd solid for inner border and squares
- 1⅓ yds outer border

BINDING
- ⅝ yd coordinating fabric

BACKING
- 4¼ yds coordinating fabric

SAMPLE QUILT
- **A New Leaf** by Mitzi Powers for Bentartex Fabrics

1 unroll & cut

Open your jelly roll carefully leaving the strips in tact just as they come off the roll.

TO MAKE THE CORNERSTONES: cut (3) 2½" strips from the solid fabric. Subcut into (42) 2½" squares.

2 sew

Start with a jelly roll strip. Add a 2½" square; to the square, a strip; followed by a square, and so on. Continue in this manner through the entire jelly roll.
YIELD: one continuous strip

Cut about 18" off the last strip. It really doesn't matter the exact measurement. This ensures your 2½" squares will appear to be placed randomly.

2 make strip

3 sew

Hold on to the end. Find the other end of your continuous strip. With both ends RST sew the strip to itself lengthwise all the way back to the fold. Cut the fold.

1 Find both ends of the continuous strip. Sew the strip to itself lengthwise back toward the fold.

2 When you get close to the fold, stop and cut the strip in half. Finish sewing.

3 The next time you will cut across two strips, and so on.

Again hold the end, find the beginning and stitch lengthwise back to the fold. Cut the fold again. Repeat.

TOTAL: 5 times. Square up.
QUILT CENTER: approx. 55" x 63"

4 borders

Cut (7) 2½" strips from the inner border fabric. Piece together strips when needed. Add top and bottom inner borders to quilt top **A** & **B**; add side borders **C** & **D**.

Cut (6) 6½" strips from outer border fabric. Add the outer borders to the quilt top in the same order as the inner borders were added.

5 quilt & bind

Layer quilt top on batting and backing and quilt the way you like. Square up all raw edges. Cut (8) 2½" strips and piece together end-to-end with diagonal seams—plus sign method. Fold in half lengthwise, press. Attach to your quilt raw edges together with a quarter inch seam allowance. Turn the folded binding edge to the back and tack in place with an invisible stitch—or machine stitch if you like.

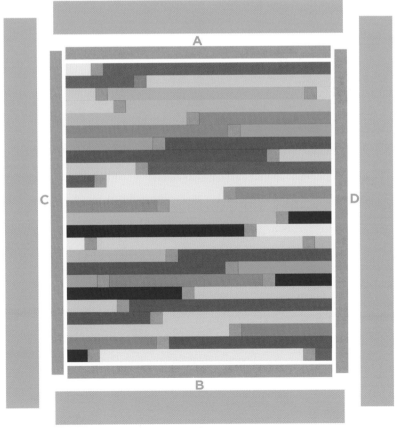

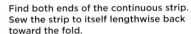

4 add borders

Garden Party
brighten your day with color

quilt designed by JENNY DOAN

I am one of those people that just chooses to be happy! When life gives you lemons you make lemonade! When life gives you scraps you make quilts, and picking fabrics for your "Garden Party" posies are the kind of choices we all like to make!

One of my happier choices came on a cold, cloudy, winter day. It had been raining for hours, and piles of what had been snow, were now slush. It clumped in puddles of mud dotting the yard and the corners of the front steps. Outside my window tiny purple crocuses poked their heads up around my front steps, ignorant of the snow and bitter weather. They seemed to be chiding me for my melancholy attitude, asking "Why are you so low? Spring is on its way!" They didn't seem to care at all, smiling on at the day that was waiting to welcome them, rain or shine!

I can't help smiling when I remember the choice they offered me. Rainy day gloom or springtime beauty! Who cares if its winter. Spring would bring more change, somewhere behind the clouds, it was on it's way.

Creating is important no matter what season, and when we can't get out and garden we can create it on our own with a sewing machine! A simple pansy comes to life using fabric and bringing that sunshine into our hearts.

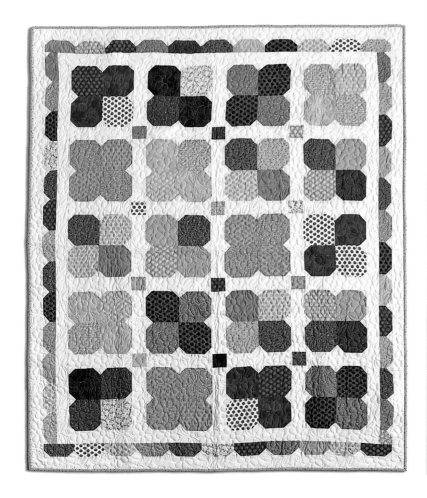

Think about those bright little faces spread across a yard or flower bed, braving the winter chill to bring us our first springtime smiles; those beautiful little flowers, pushing their way up to a lonely bed so they could claim the day and make it the best one they could! I knew just what my choice would be. I'd turn snowballs into poises and we'd have flowers that would last much longer than a season. These flowers would become an heirloom.

Creating the "Garden Party" quilt lifted my spirits and all of a sudden there were flowers everywhere! I used bright, cheerful prints that could delight you on a blustery winter day the same way they did for me.

Making this quilt is a simple way to choose to be happy. It goes together in a jiffy and is an easy way to bring a bouquet of flowers into anyone's life during any time of year.

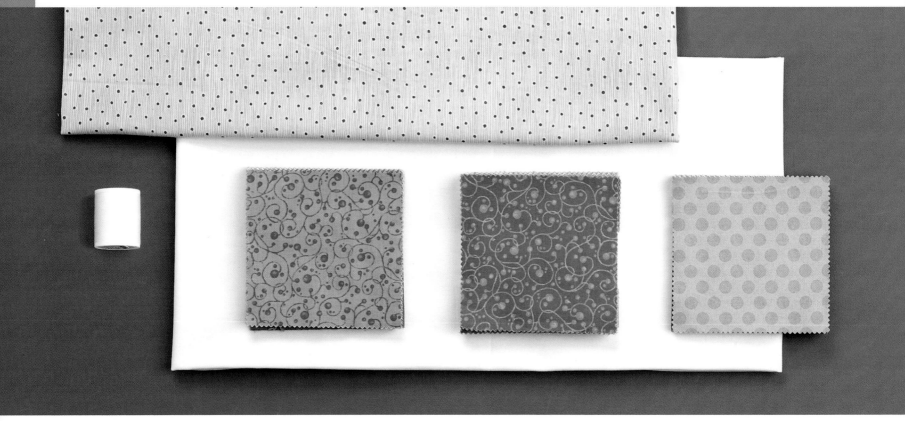

materials

make a 50" x 63" charm pack quilt

QUILT TOP
- 3 charm packs
- 1¾ yd background fabric, inner & outer borders

BINDING
- ⅝ yd coordinating fabric

BACKING
- 3¼ yds coordinating fabric

SAMPLE QUILT
- **This 'n' That** by Nancy Halvorsen for Benartex
- **Bella Solid White** by Moda Fabrics

1 group colors
Separate the lights out of the charm packs. The colors will be grouped into 4 coordinating squares for each flower. Make 20 flower groups.

2 cut
From the background fabric cut (13) 1½" strips. Subcut into 1½" squares. 240 are needed next. Set aside 96 for the pieced border.

3 snowball
Snowballing the square will make the corners appear rounded. Use (3) 1½" squares and one flower

3 snowball 3 corners
RST, sew across, trim

3 flip & press

Snowball 3 corners of each flower charm square.

Trim off excess fabric.

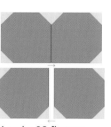

4 make 20 flowers

5 add sashing to left side of 15 blocks

Sew a sashing strip between flower blocks

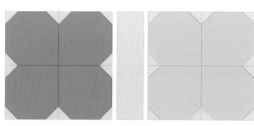

6 each row starts and ends with a flower

The cornerstone in the sashing between rows will line up with the sashing that's between blocks.

square. Place the small background squares RST on 3 corners of a flower square. Sew diagonally across. Trim off excess. Press and flip. Repeat for all 80 flower charm squares.

4 flower

Use 4 snowballed flower charms. Point all 90° square corners to the inside. Sew the top 2; then bottom 2 charms together. Pressing arrows aid in nesting seams. Attach top & bottom for one flower. Press. Make 20.

5 sashing

Cut (7) 2½" strips of background fabric. Subcut into (28) 9½" rectangles. Attach one rectangle to the left side of (15) flower blocks. As a rule press to sashing throughout.

6 rows

Lay out (15) flower blocks block without sashing to the end of each row. This results in a 4 x 5 grid layout. Sew attached in 5 rows of 3 flowers each. Add a simple flower block to complete the rows in an eye-pleasing 4 x 5 grid. Sew blocks together side-to-side.

7 sashing +

Cut (3) 5" printed charm squares in half twice to make 2½" square cornerstones. Or for a scrappier look use as many as 12 prints. Add a 2½" square to the right of (12) 9½" sashing rectangles. Sew (3) of these units end-to-end. Add a last sashing strip to a cornerstone. Make 4.

Between the flower block rows add a long sashing strip. Nest seams whenever possible. Sew all the rows together. Quilt center complete.

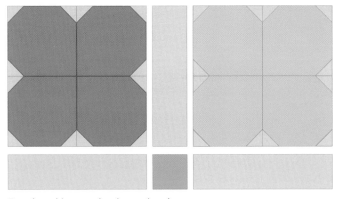

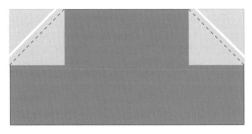

7 each sashing row begins and ends with a sashing rectangle

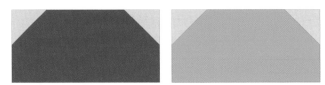

8 snowball top corners

8 piece end-to-end

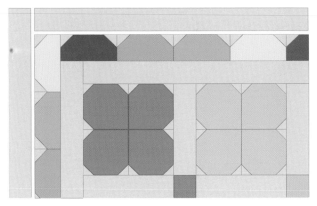

9 add outer border

8 inner border

Cut (7) 2½" strips of border fabric. Measure quilt top width. Piece strips to get the length needed and attach to top and bottom; Repeat for quilt top sides. Press to borders.

9 pieced border

With the remaining charm squares create a pieced border. Cut (24) charm squares in half. Use the (96) 1½" squares that were set aside.

Snowball the top two corners of the horizontal charm rectangles.

Lay the rectangles end-to-end and piece together to the length needed for the top and bottom of the quilt center, 11 each. Repeat for the quilt sides, about 13 each.

10 outer border

Repeat inner border steps once more.

11 quilt & bind

Layer quilt top on batting and backing and quilt the way you like. Square up all raw edges.

Cut (8) 2½" strips from binding fabric and piece together end-to-end with diagonal seams, aka plus sign method.

Fold in half lengthwise, press. Attach to your quilt raw edges together with a ¼" seam.

Turn the folded binding edge to the back and tack in place with an invisible stitch— or machine stitch if you like.

Jacob's Ladder

vintage is the new modern

quilt designed by JENNY DOAN

There is nothing as cozy as a homemade quilt. I have one that my grandma made for me years ago. She gave it to me on my 9th birthday along with a crocheted doily and a copy of the family cookbook. I felt so special getting such grown up gifts!

My grandma, being a child of the Depression, never worked with the fancy, new quilting fabrics available to us today. Instead she carefully cut and pieced together scraps of material left over from a lifetime of sewing projects. I loved to look at my quilt and find squares of my Easter dress, my Barbie doll's nightgown and countless other familiar fabrics. It was almost like a scrapbook of my childhood.

We all have warm memories of fresh-baked bread, canned peaches, and, best of all, homemade quilts.

For some reason, though, these "domestic arts" fell out of popularity for a while. I would have been hard-pressed to find a classmate who knew one thing about hemming a skirt or embroidering a pillowcase, but these days it seems like the younger generation is feeling the urge to return to their roots. As a result we are seeing a huge resurgence of all things "vintage."

Last summer I went to the wedding of a cute young couple. The reception was just adorable. The food and decor were straight out of a bridal magazine. It was obvious that the bride had spent months planning every little detail, and the result was simply stunning. But I couldn't get over how much of the wedding had an old-fashioned feel to it. Yellow lemonade was served in mason jars with orange and white striped straws. Old wooden windows had been converted into picture frames to display the bridal and engagement photos. Everywhere I looked I saw fun little touches of the past, but each with a fresh, modern twist.

It seems that vintage is the new modern. Craft blogs are filled with tutorials on how to transform old fashioned thrift store finds into stylish, one-of-a-kind pieces. Antique doors become shabby-chic headboards. Tired, old armchairs are brought back to life with an up-to-date coat of paint and trendy new upholstery. The result is a project that feels nostalgic and trendy all at once!

We love the idea of taking a traditional quilt like Jacob's Ladder and giving it a modern twist as well. What could be better than mixing the comfort of the classics with the innovation and style of today.

> " These days it seems like the younger generation is feeling the urge to return to their roots. "

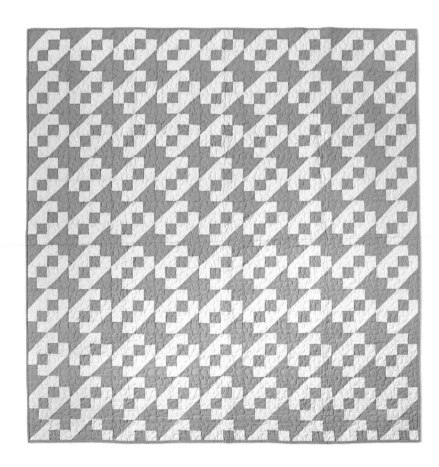

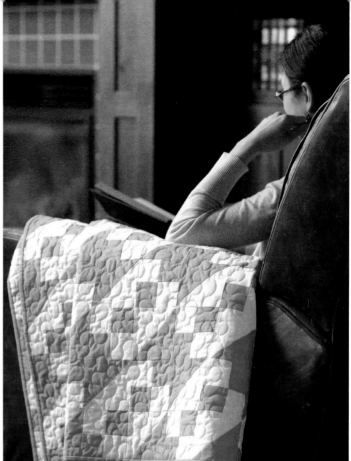

materials
makes a 68" X 73" quilt

QUILT TOP
- 1¾ yds light solid
- 1¾ yds dark solid

BINDING
- ⅝ yd coordinating fabric

BACKING
- 5½ yds coordinating fabric

SAMPLE QUILT
- **Bella Solids Bleached White** by Moda (98)
- **Bella Solids Cheddar** by Moda (152)

1 construct half square triangles

Cut (11) 5" strips from each of the dark and light fabrics. Subcut into 5" squares.

YIELD: (86) 5" squares from each color fabric.

Iron a diagonal into each light 5" square. Pair each ironed square with a dark square RST (right sides together).

With the light charm square on top, sew a standard quilting ¼" seam on either side of the ironed diagonal. Cut between the two seams. Press to the dark side. Repeat.

YIELD: 2 HSTs
TOTAL: 171

2 make 4-patch

Subcut into (86) 5" squares of each color.

With one light and one dark square RST, sew 2 opposite edges of the square.

TIP: If you don't sew across 2 colors in this step you will not get a 4-patch.

Cut in half between the two seams at 2½." Press to the dark side. Lay the two RST opposing colors, and nest the seams. Sew across the seams on opposite sides. Cut down the center between to the seams at 2½." Press.

YIELD: (2) 4-patch blocks.
Make 171

TIP: For greater success, square up your HSTs so they equal the size of the 4-patch blocks before you begin this next step.

3 layout

A large flat surface comes in handy when laying out blocks in their correct order and orientation. Basically, the two rows repeat over and over.

All the 4-patches in this quilt need to be laid out **exactly** the same. The HSTs, however, will change orientation from row to row.

Begin row 1 with a 4-patch. Whichever direction you place the HST—light on top for example—repeat the same direction for the entire row, 18 blocks in all.

Begin row 2 with an HST but switch orientations–dark on top. Continue odd and even rows in this fashion. 19 rows in total.

1 After sewing on either side of the center fold, cut between stitching lines. Yield: 2 HSTs

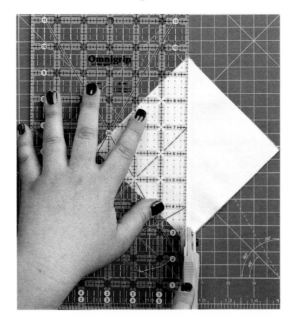

2 After sewing on two opposing outside edges, cut the squares in half between the seams.

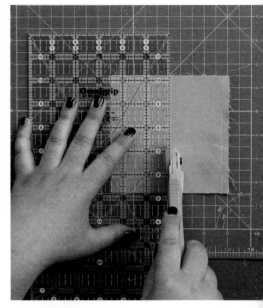

3 An easy way to nest your seams is to press to the dark side. This will allow the seams to naturally come together. Also, you can take the two middles and rub with your fingers to feel them align.

4 Again cut down the middle between the two seams.

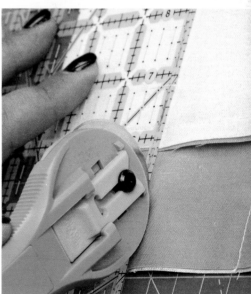

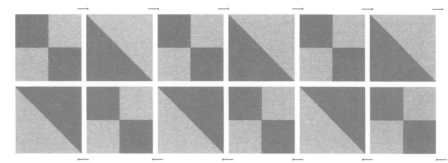

3 layout grid: 18 x 19; all 4-patches same; HSTs change from row to row

4 sew

Sew each block to the next across to build rows. Press all seams to one side on even rows; to the opposite side on odd rows. This will help with nesting. See arrows.

Sew all rows together, nesting seams as you go and pressing seams to the bottom.

5 quilt & bind

Layer quilt top on batting and backing and quilt the way you like. Square up all raw edges.

Cut (8) 2½″ strips of binding. Piece together with diagonal seams.

Fold in half WST lengthwise, press. Attach to your quilt raw edges together with a ¼″ seam allowance.

Turn the folded binding edge to the back and tack in place with an invisible stitch–or machine stitch if you like.

TERMS:
HST: half square triangle
WST: wrong sides together
RST: right sides together

4 sew blocks together to make a row; rows together to build the quilt

Attaching a hanging sleeve

to the back of your quilt

Attaching a hanging sleeve before the quilt is bound starts by measuring the width of your quilted quilt. You will need a piece of fabric that measures eight inches wide. The length will equal the width of your quilt top minus two inches. For example, if your quilt is 50 inches wide, you will need a piece of fabric that measures 48 x 8 inches.

Finish the 8" ends of this strip by turning the edge under and hemming it. You could also serge the edge if desired.

Fold the strip in half lengthwise and press. Attach it lengthwise to the top edge of your quilt along with the binding. There will be several layers: quilt, sleeve and binding in that order. The important thing is that all raw edges are aligned. Sew through all layers at once with a quarter inch seam allowance. The binding will then flip over to cover the seam.

Pin the bottom of the sleeve in place on your quilt back. Begin with a couple of anchoring stitches. Then hand stitch the folded edge to the back of your quilt. Make sure that the needle doesn't go through the quilt, you won't want these stitches showing on the front.

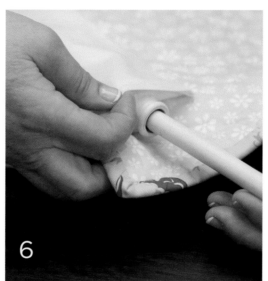

Don't worry if your quilt is already bound, you can still add a sleeve to the back. Just take that same 8 inch strip, finish the short ends. Then sew the strip lengthwise right sides together making a tube. Flip right side out. Press the tube with the seam centered down the middle. Pin along the top edge of your quilt, and hand sew both folded lengths using a hidden binding stitch.

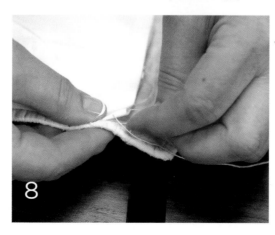

TIP: *If you wish to reduce stress on the quilt, attach a sleeve to both the top and bottom of the quilt. Then you can flip your quilt regularly. This will reduce the wear and strain on your quilt.*

Attaching a label

to the back of your quilt

There are many options available for adding a label to your quilt. Labeling your quilt can be as easy as signing your quilt with a permanent marker. But there are many options available. There are many pre-made labels to choose from, or you can make your own with a small piece of leftover fabric from your project. You could even iron on a patch. One of our favorite ways to add a label is to attach it to the bottom corner of the quilt catching it in the binding.

Finish the two sides of your label that will not be caught in the binding. Pin it in place and hand stitch around the finished edges attaching it to your quilt. Now when you stitch the binding into place you will be enclosing the raw edges of your label. We recommend writing your message on your fabric before you do the stitching. Jenny says, "If you make a mistake you can try again on a new piece of fabric." You could also embroider the message either by hand or with an embroidery machine. You can also label your quilt before quilting and it will become a permanent part of your quilt.

Some things you may want to include on your label

- Who the quilt is for
- Who made the quilt
- The date
- The occasion
- The pattern
- Who quilted the quilt

91

disap-
pearing
pinwheel
shoofly

DESIGNED BY
Jenny Doan

PIECED BY
Jenny Doan

QUILTED BY
Betty Bates

QUILT SIZE
75 ¾" x 87"

QUILT TOP
1 layer cake print
1 layer cake bkgnd solid
1 ¼ yd border fabric solid

BINDING
⅝ yd coordinating fabric

BACKING
5 yds coordinating fabric

FABRIC USED
Floral Gatherings by
Primitive Gatherings
for Moda Fabrics

Bella Solids Natural by
Moda Fabrics

ONLINE TUTORIALS
msqc.co/Shoofly

QUILTING
Loops and Swirls

disap-
pearing
pinwheel
churn
dash

DESIGNED BY
Jenny Doan

PIECED BY
Jenny Doan

QUILTED BY
Betty Bates

QUILT SIZE
57" X 68"

QUILT TOP
1 layer cake
1 yd outer border

BINDING
⅝ yd coordinating fabric

BACKING
3½ yds coordinating fabric

FABRIC USED
Muslin Mates by Moda
Fabrics

ONLINE TUTORIALS
msqc.co/ChurnDash

QUILTING
Paisley Feathers

falling charm

DESIGNED BY
Jenny Doan

PIECED BY
Stephen Nixdorf

QUILTED BY
Jamey Stone

QUILT SIZE
83" X 96"

QUILT TOP
4 charm packs **OR** 1 layer cake
2 jelly rolls bkgnd solid

BINDING
¾ yd coordinating fabric

BACKING
7½ yds coordinating fabric

FABRIC USED
Weave by Moda Fabrics

Bella Solids Silver
by Moda Fabrics (9900 183)

ONLINE TUTORIALS
msqc.co/Falling

QUILTING
Square Meander

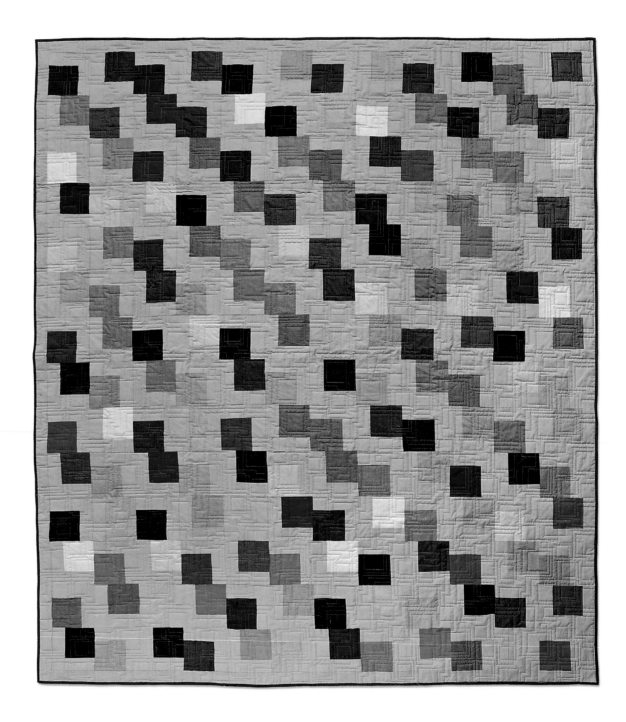

freestyle star

DESIGNED BY
Natalie Earnheart

PIECED BY
Natalie Earnheart

QUILTED BY
Kathleen Miller

QUILT SIZE
65" X 71"

QUILT TOP
1 layer cake white
1 layer cake print
1¼ yd outer border

BINDING
⅝ yd coordinating fabric

BACKING
4 yds coordinating fabric

TOOLS
MSQC large wedge ruler

FABRIC USED
True Colors by Joel
Dewberry for Free Spirit
Fabrics

Bella Solid White by Moda
Fabrics

ONLINE TUTORIALS
msqc.co/Freestyle

QUILTING
Cotton Seed

garden
party

DESIGNED BY
Jenny Doan

PIECED BY
Cassie Nixdorf

QUILTED BY
Adrian Stacey

QUILT SIZE
50" x 63"

QUILT TOP
3 charm packs
1¾ yd background fabric,
inner & outer borders

BINDING
⅝ yd coordinating fabric

BACKING
3¼ yds coordinating fabric

FABRIC USED
This 'n' That by Nancy
Halvorsen for Benartex

Bella Solid White by Moda
Fabrics

ONLINE TUTORIALS
msqc.co/GardenParty

QUILTING
Flowers

jacob's ladder

DESIGNED BY
Jenny Doan

PIECED BY
Jenny Doan

QUILTED BY
Kathleen Miller

QUILT SIZE
68" X 73"

QUILT TOP
1¾ yds light solid
1¾ yds dark solid

BINDING
¾ yd coordinating fabric

BACKING
5½ yds coordinating fabric

FABRIC USED
Bella Solids by Moda
Fabrics

Bleached White 9900 98
Cheddar 9900 152

ONLINE TUTORIALS
msqc.co/Jacobs

QUILTING
Meander

jelly roll race 2

DESIGNED BY
Sarah Galbraith

PIECED BY
Cassie Nixdorf

QUILTED BY
Adrian Stacey

QUILT SIZE
71" X 79"

QUILT TOP
1 jelly roll
1 yd solid for inner border and squares
1⅓ yds outer border

BINDING
⅝ yd coordinating fabric

BACKING
4¾ yds coordinating fabric

FABRIC USED
A New Leaf by Mitzi Powers for Bentartex fabrics

ONLINE TUTORIALS
msqc.co/JellyRace

QUILTING
Curly Twirly Flower

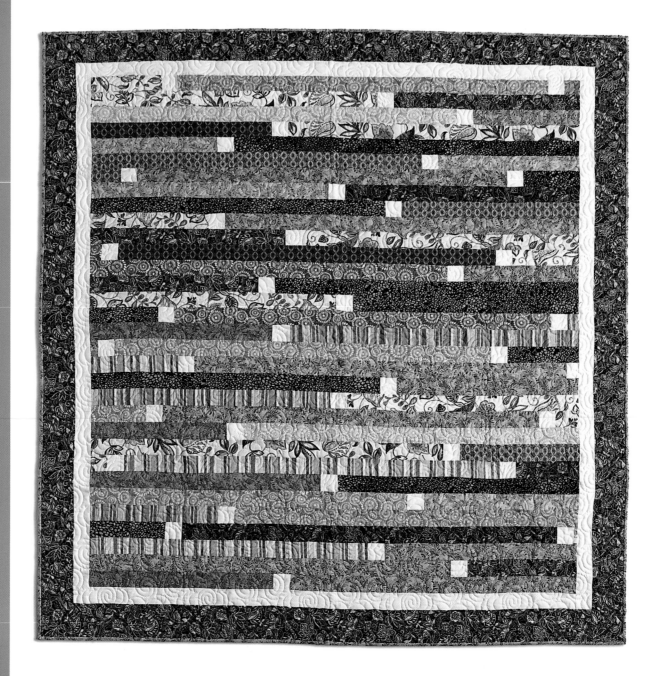

love notes

DESIGNED BY
Natalie Earnheart

PIECED BY
Cindy Morris

QUILTED BY
Emma Jensen

QUILT SIZE
39" x 50"

QUILT TOP
1 printed charm pack
1 bkgnd solid charm pack
⅜ yd bkgnd solid inner border
¾ yd outer border

BINDING
½ yd coordinating fabric

BACKING
1⅝ yds coordinating fabric

FABRIC USED
Surrounded By Love
by Deb Strain for
Moda Fabrics

Bella Solids Bleached White
by Moda Fabrics

ONLINE TUTORIALS
msqc.co/LoveNotes

QUILTING
Hearts Large

lattice

DESIGNED BY
Jenny Doan

PIECED BY
Jenny Doan

QUILTED BY
Kathleen Miller

QUILT SIZE
71" x 67"

QUILT TOP
4 charm packs **OR** 1 layer cake
1 honey bun solid for lattice **OR** 1¾ yd solid for lattice
1 yd outer border

BINDING
⅝ yd coordinating fabric

BACKING
4 yds coordinating fabric

FABRIC USED
Front Porch by Jan Patek for Moda Fabrics

ONLINE TUTORIALS
msqc.co/Lattice

QUILTING
Daisy Days

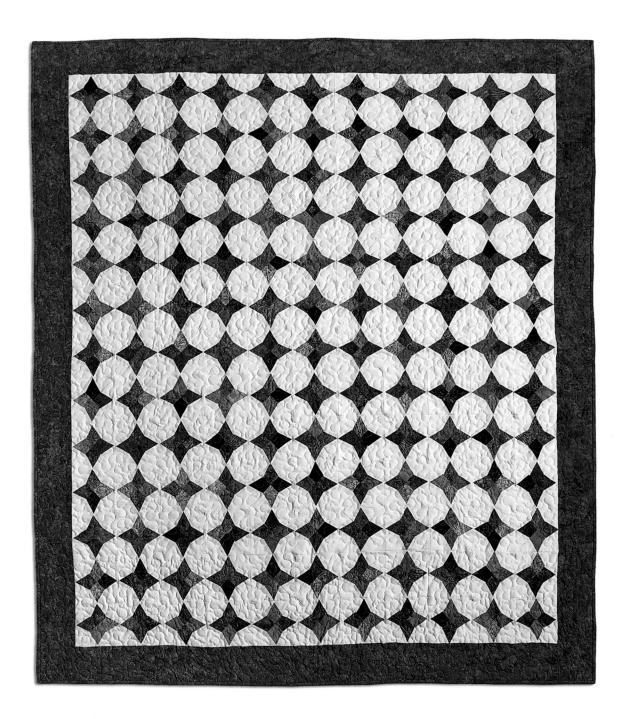

mini periwinkle

DESIGNED BY
Natalie Earnheart

PIECED BY
Stephen & Cassie Nixdorf

QUILTED BY
Adrian Stacey

QUILT SIZE
67" x 77"

QUILT TOP
1 jelly roll for periwinkles
OR 4 charm packs
7½ yds bkgnd fabric
1 yd outer border

BINDING
⅝ yd coordinating fabric

BACKING
4¼ yds coordinating fabric

FABRIC USED
Lagoon Batiks by RJR

Bella Solids White by
Moda Fabrics (9900 98)

TOOLS
MSQC mini wacky web
template tool

MSQC small triangle
papers (3 packets)

ONLINE TUTORIALS
msqc.co/Periwinkle

QUILTING
Meander

wonky star

DESIGNED BY
Natalie Earnheart

PIECED BY
Natalie Earnheart

QUILTED BY
Jamey Stone

QUILT SIZE
66" X 77"

QUILT TOP
1 layer cake with duplicates
of each fabric* **OR** 1 layer
cake and 1 charm pack of
the same collection
1 layer cake solid
¾ yd inner border
1½ yd outer border

BINDING
¾ yd coordinating fabric

BACKING
4 yds coordinating fabric

FABRIC USED
Belle by Amy Butler for
Rowan Fabrics (*only 1
layer cake needed)

ONLINE TUTORIALS
msqc.co/Wonky

QUILTING
Bo Dangle

- All seams are ¼" inch unless directions specify differently.

- Cutting instructions are given at the point when cutting is required.

- Precuts are not prewashed; therefore do not prewash other fabrics in the project

- All strips are cut WOF

- Remove all selvedges

- All yardages based on 40" WOF

ACRONYMS USED

MSQC	Missouri Star Quilt Co.
RST	right sides together
WST	wrong sides together
HST	half square triangle
WOF	width of fabric
LOF	length of fabric

pre-cut glossary

CHARM PACK

1 = (42) 5" squares or ¾ yd of fabric
1 = baby
2 = crib
3 = lap
4 = twin

JELLY ROLL

1 = (42) 2½" strips cut the width of fabric
    or 2¾ yds of fabric
1 = a twin
2 = queen

LAYER CAKE

1 = (42) 10" squares of fabric: 2¾ yds total
1 = a twin
2 = queen

The terms charm pack, jelly roll, and layer cake are trademarked names that belong to Moda. Other companies use different terminology, but the sizes remain the same.

When we mention a precut, we are basing the pattern on a 40-42 count pack. Not all precuts have the same count, so be sure to check the count on your precut to make sure you have enough pieces to complete your project.

press seams

- Use a steam iron on the cotton setting.

- Iron the seam just as it was sewn RST. This "sets" the seam.

- With dark fabric on top, lift the dark fabric and press back.

- The seam allowance is pressed to the dark side. Some patterns may direct otherwise for certain situations.

- Follow pressing arrows in the diagrams when indicated.

- Press toward borders. Pieced borders may demand otherwise.

- Press diagonal seams open on binding to reduce bulk.

binding

- Use 2½" strips for binding.

- Sew strips end-to-end into one long strip with diagonal seams, aka plus sign method (next). Press seams open.

- Fold in half lengthwise WST and press.

- The entire length should equal the outside dimension of the quilt plus 15" - 20".

plus sign method

Diagonal seams are used when straight seams would add too much bulk.

- Lay one strip across the other as if to make a plus sign RST.

- Sew from top inside to bottom outside corners crossing the intersections of fabric as you sew. Trim excess to ¼" seam allowance.

- Press seam open.

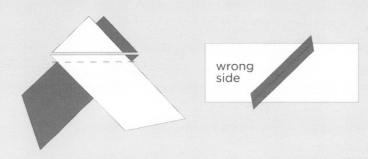

wrong side

attach binding

- Match raw edges of folded binding to the quilt top edge.

- Leave a 10" tail at the beginning.

- Use a ¼" seam allowance.

- Start in the middle of a long straight side.

miter binding corners

- Stop sewing ¼" before the corner.
- Move the quilt out from under the pressure foot.
- Clip the threads.
- Flip the binding up at a 90° angle to the edge just sewn.
- Fold the binding down along the next side to be sewn.
- Align the fold to the edge of the quilt that was *just sewn*;
- Align raw edges to the side *to be sewn*.
- Begin sewing on the fold.

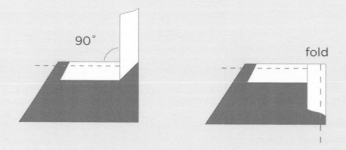

*MSQC recommends **The Binding Tool** from TQM Products to finish binding perfectly every time.*

close binding

- Stop sewing when you have 12" left to reach the start.

- Leave a 10" tail; trim binding if necessary.

- It helps to pin or clip the quilt together at the two points where the binding starts and stops. This takes the pressure off of the binding tails while you work.

- Where binding comes together overlap 2½" or the width of your binding. Trim.

- Use the plus sign method to sew the two binding ends together, except this time when making the plus sign, match the edges and sew across. If you need to, mark your sewing line with a pencil since you won't see where the corners intersect.

- Trim off excess; press seam open.

- Fold in half WST and align all raw edges to the quilt top.

- Sew binding closed. Press.

- Turn the folded edge of the binding around to the back of the quilt and tack into place with an invisible stitch or machine stitch if you wish.

borders

- Always measure the quilt center 3 times before cutting borders.

- Start with the width and measure the top edge, middle and bottom.

- Folding the quilt in half is a quick way to find the middle.

- Take the average of those 3 measurements.

- Cut 2 border strips to that size.

- Attach one to the top; one to the bottom of the quilt.

- Position the border fabric on top as you sew. The feed dogs can act like rufflers. Having the border on top will prevent waviness and keep the quilt straight.

- Repeat this process for the side borders, measuring the length 3 times.

- Include the newly attached top and bottom borders in your measurements.

- Press to the borders.